Between First & Second Sleep

Between
First & Second
Sleep

Tamsin Spencer Smith

fmʃbw

San Francisco, California

"Encounters" was commissioned for a forthcoming Hieronymus Bosch and Pieter Breugel anthology, as a response to Bosch's altarpiece fragment "Christ Carrying the Cross" with "Christ Child with Walking Frame" on the reverse, at the Museum of Art History in Vienna, Austria;

"Maroon Bells" appeared as a broadside (Aspen, CO: The Aspen Institute, 2018);

"An Invitation" appeared as a broadside (Emeryville, CA: Western Editions, 2018);

"Totality" was first published in the verse collection "Reverberations: A Visual Conversation" (Sebastopol, CA: Risk Press, 2018).

Cover drawing by Emilio Villalba

Author photo by Matt Gonzalez

San Francisco, California

To Scully and Tabitha
& to all the makers

CONTENTS

HOW TO PAINT FROM LIFE

I am alone
in shared space
arranging fruit
a requisite bouquet
dried and tied by wool
yarn or ruched ribbon
one glass half-full
I drank the other
half which oddly honors
part of the plan
today's lesson being
things as they are
so I return to the staged
scene set in staged light
to study perspective
discern true colors
by looking through
a cardboard view
hole-punched to pinpoint
value hue by hue
for what the mind
sees as red
is often kind of blue
in tone
vivid or faint
a life all its own
self-contained and free
to glaze the rest
in spectral play
proof truth easily seen
is especially susceptible
to seduction
as apples glow
more vibrant
after their ruddy fall

AUTOMATIC DRAWING
for Ed Wiener

I want
clear as gravity
casual as it is complex
like a mouth that becomes
itself only by mobilizing
positive and negative
space into motion
a spiral love
a cloud love
an uncut single wire
turned and bent
softened to form
bowl, fish, water
bare whole infinite breath

HOW TO WRITE

There are words
to wash out
sunny plans
quench fire
feed drought
some seek the chase
or beg to roam
your animal insides
pace the cage
claw the bars
trail indigo
across the blotter
you let them
escape

LANDSCAPE OF THE SMALL HOURS

1 A.M.
I am aroused
by dark remembrance
a small child sniffling
unconsoled and forgotten
on her school stairwell
while I remain
a single chair floating in a garden
uncertain where to turn
the mess I've been working
paint stroke and dab
to push without losing
the something it already has
its outlined life
without backing or place to rest
would detail make it any less
recognizable or out its anomaly
there in the middle of nowhere
intrinsically smearing hints
of the nature of things
for the little girl wails anew
she too is reworking
from the inside
I hang my head
from the window call out
again but still she can't hear
it's so late or too early
to sleep in peace
might I place her
there with hints of mad flower
and green upon the seatless frame
light as sky lighter
than linseed or wishing
one's own abstraction
could save the bees
or those we cherish

ZEST
for Kim Frohsin

The artist told us her tale about lemons
An instance of resistance
She poured into paint
So now when I look
At the luscious sliced orbs and admire
The skillful enamel of the dotted French knife
My forearm tickles with the feel of
Juice running down and I don't care
Because I meant that to be
A reason for my love to lick me
There or later at the bottom
Of a *one last kiss* stair
Where it was I can't recall
But I've heard that one should roll lemons
Back and forth with some pressure
To get the most of what's within
The fleshy pulp
The pith beneath
Unhurried skin
The wait which has far outlasted the man
She never went to bed with anyhow

OTHERLAND BESIDES

Feverish in between
First sleep and second

Sense wrestles
Over thinking

Veers stoically
Beyond certain

Election to embrace
Non-chasing

Animal quiet
Within

The continent of self
Divides a peace

Sequels of columned life
From teeming deep

Sediment and strata
Sheets

Tangled above
Sweet marine bed

Topography shifts
Weather will pass

If first a plunge to land
Then gradually a slope

Of nature
One docks

Two wrestle
Clear of clock

Sheep counting
Or backward grasping

At last
Awake

EN PLEIN AIR

Scene opens
In repose upon my easel
Southern light sets
Sea-side semblance
And an island beyond
Twilight's tease
All that fades upon arrival
A spring that empties
The self set bare
Lets feeling invade the fore
We cannot know which classical order
Propels our composition
Life knifes into view as with waves
It is important to illustrate tension
Likening silhouettes of the unsaid
To surrounds that don't know their place
I have had such dreams

A POEM OF WEIGHTS & MEASURES
after Instagram

Another night's scroll
Through tender shares
A couple in Paris snaps
Anubis escorting the dead
Three thousand years of remembering
It's never too late for grace
Or to show oneself how
The public passion of a sunset reveals
Even a vendor's neon sign can
Heart-alter an offer
We are betrayed by flashing arrows
No emoji can contain
My friend is never coming back
Only closer in a close-up
Shots of a Sunday drive
California's Coast the star
And others bowling alone
In middling airports anonymous
Shapes race soggy dogs
Back to fractured shores
There are emotional reactions
For all of these events
And mood multiples
Creatively out-put
Details revealed
Of selves in progress
Interior mirrors
#nofilter

ANTIDOTE, CYANOTYPE, & VINCENT VAN GOGH'S *STARRY NIGHT*

What couldn't a kid do with 152 assorted crayons
Arrayed for easy view
In their brand-new ultimate carry case
No eye's too wide when kaleidoscope's your parachute
Replete with full metallic range and bonus glitter-blends
All at finger's tip
      wrapped in coachable safe-words
            to gloss any slip

      For why should innocent offspring suffer
The burden of bygone scarcity or curse
Manifest acts that
Skin honor raw or worse

      For *Flesh* can be made *Peach*
But should we not fear forgetting
The big and the little errors
That cannot be rubbed away

      In a Cold War fit
We dissed a clever begetter *Prussian Blue*
To usher an era of *Wide Blue Yonder*
So no child need unwittingly draw iron curtains

      It's the modern way to revise yesterday
Ditch the counterculture wanderlust of *Dandelion*
Welcome *Inchworm* to the pantheon
As a dirt-free green that makes dreaming pristine

I bear no nostalgia for bad decisions
Past crimes and things no child would want to know
But I am made nervous by the renaming of history
The burial of monuments to our stupidity

Must we not
Decide what to do
With our ground-down nibs

To keep
Or throw away
To color within
Or over the lines

OF PERFECT TEMPERATURE

for Mary Julia Klimenko

I order a tea
Called *exuberant*
Waiting for you

Bystanders steer
Me to *buttery cloud*
Or *mango mist*

Well, without the try
How could I know
Whether oolong's my type

What fates the leaves would bring
Entering alleyways
Brighter lights

In laughter
We pass words
Like oxygen

Drop smiles
In cups
As fortunes

AVANT BUS STOP

for Peter Hirshberg

things pulled from the lost and found
crab legs and turquoise moss
beastly chess pieces galloping in sealed plastic
table tennis and everything felt
spray paint newsprint
unwinding as a toy
or who could forget the bronzed face
with the macaroni smile
nameless footprints frame
the expectation of escape
mounting block by block
backed by grey rucksack
a door swings
the newcomer bites into a coin
gives the rest to you
a token
before it becomes a toll
hurry a door
is closing

LA DOLCE VITA

Crowds innocent of aspect
assemble their arial shapes
so stars long-dead may remember
their break from fixed intangible
to free and falling

For what's right in front of us
so often hardest to see
is missed when we look
too late at last for the ancient
face among the ruins

Flashing sky-pennies
splash in night's fountain
oh, to be in Rome again
a wet and glinting force
for well wishing

I am not lost
infinite nor treasured
chest tender from so much opening
but why close eyes
to make one wish come true?

Light such as ours would never
dare dispelled a spell's spark
we should be clear
about suffering
cease mumbling

Strange days
dear enough
even now
to shorten up the distance
what mind wills and nerves allow

Let us plunge
cataclysmic

———

nostalgic fools
running towards

Our own reflections
beckoning be
good life
be sweet

MOON MONOCHROME
after the fires

Prodigy child of the jalousie smile
Accompany the beat of rain's relentless argument
So each shadow soliloquy itself simply accepts

By scattering the glories of white morning
Instruments of quiet liaison opening
The envelope of earliest sound

Who is to hear the timbre of forest
Who scales the wake of cinder
A knowing older than memory

The hand which once bent metal
Lifts a crystal jar from dry ash
Behold the artist's frosted heart perennial

Spirit of all nocturne
Melody and broken chord
Suspended. Complete.

Night-blooming
As bright fantastic keys
Swimming through an amber sky

Frederic Chopin's body is buried in Paris, where he died in 1849. At his request, his heart was removed, encased in a jar of cognac, and smuggled past Russian authorities into what is now Poland. During the Warsaw Uprising of 1944, occupying German forces stole the heart and hid it away from rallying nationalists. They feared the composer's symbolic importance to the Polish people.

DECLARATION OF OUR DISCOVERY

Because yes
may be only partly
animal attraction
chemical reaction
or edible phrase
the vine of the mind
cannot divine manufactured sound
as anything other than confusing
some sign that hope frowns
at the secondary embrace
of a hinged parenthetical
the rut of either-neither
open nor shut about
to fold the corner on
some unknown beyond
where we never have
before been but hold
as skin cradles rib
reforms a split
or as with delicacy plucked
the tree gives
quicker than
a bruise conspires
to map retreat
for there ever
is and was never
more than only one
first wet bite
to teach what to seek
for it is not the fruit
but the yen to reach
that moves the hand
& dares all lips
to the meaning
of all mornings

STUDIO PRACTICE

meet me
in the green corner
window where loose
space takes whatever day
lights on offer and alley
sounds and school sounds
just about approximate
a story circle unconscious
of its exquisite indirection
oral tradition plus
post-modern manifestation
a just harmless human coterie
glossing one to the next
sans axiom or assertion
proverb or law
eavesdropping
we trade a boxed lunch
with one fork
barely noting
it all comes back around, right?
the sense that transcends data
the window opening another
epic to each common allusion
thoroughly ours and loved
by each unmetered hour
in this small sacred room
full of why

LOST SAILOR
for the sculptor

He cannot now remember
Who knew all the naked body hides
Never having drawn your face

Except to meet his in darkness
Under cover of archetype skin
Aglow from prying public eye

We must imagine wandering all these years
In presence of statuary or running sound
His palms surge with the current of memory

Conceit of stone and river
The universal exception
Love and loss laid down

Only to begin
Unveiling disappearance
Long afternoons in the tall tall grass

CHASM

Sun lifts
Her gown
To the mouth of the river

Open water
Insensible horizon
Sound loom stirs

The metal abstinence of grain
The rumoring wind

RUMORING WIND

It is important not to romanticize
Almonds of another time
Olive, clove, bitter green
Twigs of a broken vine
Woven not to absolve
Limes left without water
Waiting warm afternoons
In the glare of
Seven red suns
Dark birds
Other shadows

Refugees of today
We are not wandering

When was the last time you bit down
Hard on the fruit of anything
Anything at all
Wanting to taste
What belongs
Do you know
Where you come from
Who will you outlast
Like you were put here to do so
Like your rough eyes could close
Forever on the fragrance
Tart to the tongue
Juice of oranges
Blood orange
Tambourines
Held out like platters

DICTIONARY OF SUPERSTITIONS

at twelve noon in complete silence
or midnight pressing
gold blade to a certain lock
the blue flowering of time
long considered travels
invisible surrender
plants harbingers
bestowed or carried
secure as *chicory*
an obstacle gift

should this happen
when halfway down or up
whistle or sit cross way
back straightforward to the day
of vulnerable fingers
encountering a moment
absolutely safe for suggestion
narrow but according
stairs in flight
themselves
to the end
surprisingly
the same direction

age-old fear
deflecting domestic
anger of gods
foolhardy seconds
never twice striking
the body demonstrably
opening flash
of ash doors
windows years
but how may miles
just enough
in gratitude
on close inspection

to shape feathers
arrowheads and folklore
silken words rewarded
with luck also a good idea
attraction of great strength
and magical allowing
you are *lightning*

FLIGHT OF THE ENCHANTER
for Lucien Shapiro

Clumsy breeze
by your side or
bird forward-moving
indications will remain
rocked by rising tides
we may stumble yet
upon sites unseen
by those who thieve
marching blithely by
a crash of casual orchestras
grass slanting through cracks
thumbed-over books
bathed in wayside bins
the trash of a smash & grab
world will withstand all
when reclaimed as shields
studded by shattered street
petals soften by storm
a barrier broken
between us no tears lost
only diamonds for the scooping
of all todays
& Wednesday
no longer too far away

C TO G HARMONY

for Charles Gonzalez

a wild bull barrels
down a cracked arroyo
the boy of eight wonders
where the silver minnows go
below the packed mud sound box
where low notes lift
from the friction of long tails

the boy that is you turns homeward
sparks in your ears
like electric echoes
pushing through the undertow
static on the radio charged by
a thick and massive blast of metal wings
they rip past trailing devilish tritones

the buzz of dissident drones
dressed as black seraphim
pull at a curtain of midnight blue
the future tense of you storms the stage
your mask is covered with stars
you take it off
your face is covered with stars

you begin to play
a song of self soliloquy
alternating currents, direct currents
AC/DC
pedal points resolving
since the day
you threw your toys away

CONVEX COMPLEX

Dear reader
objects may appear
draw closer
meaning is invisible
until exhaled
as a more or less wordless
condensation of curiosity
communicated across
emotional escarpments
unclosable as any gap
until crossed or filled
freely between
spilled contents
& heaped keepings
as per old atelier drawers
where everything is labeled
nothing is grasped
a glance in the mirror
behind glass
greetings
stranger

BEE SMOKER
for Christa Assad

Toss it all in
Keeper of the bag
You know the weight of westerly calm
When clipped to the gentlest
Hinge holds a kind of dander
More patient than breath
Or laic psalm
White palm on grey clay
Drawn to new ways
Seeing behind
Blue suits and walled cities
The Dada platypus makes its home
When the work is not good enough
Turn the slip inward
Bring something back

LA GENERALA

she of the subtle body
befriender of plants
and revolution

bravely no smaller
in a village of sharks
surrounded by false questions

would you if you could
choose the abandoning
crush of the yellow flower

from one who could not
dress uniform thoughts
standing naked for nothing

secondly and wherefore
attired in peaceful rags
wanders *perdida*

answers
amarilla
        dove   dove

CUBIST SPRING

transparent genius of the raindrop dangling
time's own pocket watch before the sundial
seasons and second hands spellbound
by the veiled shade of sleeping beauties

glassed in silent forest breeze beginning
the spiral vagrant slip of sap
mutinous as a sailor knocking back
the stale beer of stormwave winter

dip, cheer some
slow internal motor hums
May-mad raw-branched
anonymous, insatiable

a geometric spiritself
depth-whittled
defined by intersecting line
yet undefied, alone

as water is mere color
until we add the fish
disc rising from the east
west rhyming birds

flown in musical notation
through sandbag and sawdust
instinct reified
to fluent whole

for she was the siren
of the song she sang
you a zephyr of flowering rain
astride the scent of hyacinth

OBSERVATIONAL DRAWING

Books set askew, a long-handled net, dark liquid in a translucent glass, and something glinty (perhaps brass or silver slightly tarnished) on a table covered with delicate embroidered cloth.

For the ferry ride, I was told to wear a long skirt so as not to offend the local population; we disembarked, stopping first at a museum of military history, on our way to the spice sellers of the Casbah.

Something out of a Merchant Ivory film – that's how a friend described my father. Picture him, forceps in-hand, explaining the need to relax the insect specimen under damp paper towels, as a necessary step before pinning a butterfly, whose fragile body would otherwise be too brittle to spread and set without damage.

So, I'm not going to state the name of the battle. You'd accuse me of taking poetic license (and I'm conflict-averse). Suffice it to say the broad outlines align; the young man who took us through the miniature recreation of a densely forested Ardennes explained the position of the allies under surprise attack, while pressing his loosely robed body against me too embarrassed to move or cry out.

The angle of light is critical when attempting to approach veracity with oil paint. Especially, still life.

It's always been something of a joke that the first adult conversation my father and I ever had arrived at the end of my college career, and only then because Vladimir Nabokov was also a lepidopterist.

Did I mention why the topic came up?

I try not to overuse certain charged words – luminous, heart, spirit. Language too needs relaxing.

In this case, iridescence is the correct label. The precise quality that fades to the touch. The delicate scales transfer to the sweat of our skin, losing their pristine loveliness on the wing.

My college thesis was titled: *The Beastliness and Beauty of Art in Vladimir Nabokov's Novels.*

And the rest is rust and stardust.

EGGS IN A CARTON

I'm visiting friends in Todos Santos. They've driven up the track from their *casita* to meet me in town. We wander into Valle de Guadalupe for dinner at *Tres Galine*. I wonder whether there's a quip to be had from three hens crossing the road. Or better yet, an inside joke to close the miles between me and my absent love. Before I left, he and I bought a pair of paintings by Mary Robinson. *Eggs in a Carton on a Box*. One painting face-on, the other in profile. Thick visible brush work. Bitable. That morning he'd sent me a photo of eggs. I sent back a snapshot of bleached cow skulls. A duet in hard shells and fragile centers.

Over dinner, I tell my hosts Jess and Nick the story of how we'd met at a reading. *Your poems are like pastries. I want to put them in my mouth.* Jess and Nick tell me their love story. They met caretaking a man called Copper Top, who used to ride his motorcycle through Northern California in a crested copper helmet, with a sidecar full of roosters. Before he died, Copper Top replaced the sidecar with a casket he lined in velvet and rhinestone. Nick says that people came from miles around on the day of the funeral procession. I picture the crowd and see right off that the painter Bill Wheeler would have been there.

Bill was a hero in those parts and father to my friend Raspberry Hummingbird Sundown Wheeler, named for the things Bill saw when he delivered her using instructions from the Chicago Fireman's Manual. Jess says the most delicious water she's ever tasted runs through Bill Wheeler's ranch. Why am I ever surprised by the smallness of the world?

Nick and Jess know Raspberry. They know the story that Governor Reagan tried to shut down Wheeler Ranch back in the day. They know other people born there, dogs buried, couples married, and they too got the news that Bill died of Parkinson's a few weeks ago.

One of Bill's paintings hangs on my wall. A small spray of purple irises. Raspberry told me she loves that series of paintings, though they make her sad. All the real-life irises dried up when the wife who'd planted and tended them with that delicious water moved out.

Iris was a Greek goddess. She delivered messages for the gods and from the Underworld, using rainbows to move between Heaven and Earth. One way to think of buying art at auction is that you're giving beauty a second chance, another lap in the light. Bill's iris painting was a gift from my love. A gem won at auction. That's how it came to live with me.

The day before I arrived in Todos Santos, Nick's father had moved from Oregon to stay for good. He's ninety years old. It was just the three of us dining the other night at *Tres Galine*. Nick's dad had already eaten. Even so, Nick carefully cut his portions in half to share with the man he hadn't shared a roof with since he was six years old. Their family roots are Greek. Papadopoulos. Poulos is a common patronymic suffix also used as a term of endearment. In Latin *pullus*, means "nestling" or "chick." Nick refers to all his friends as *familia*, but he and Jess are ready to start one of their own. I think Copper Top would make a good nickname for a red-headed child.

ASSEMBLAGE

A man places an antique iron on a small section he's been working to keep it from curling. He cuts another long strip from a bag of monochromatic scraps he has trimmed and sorted.

He can imagine making a more artful world from the one others throw away. Sees litter line streets with possibility. Found silver mined from beer cartons, alabaster split from the shoulders of cigarette packs. Dead ends paved with green.

Glue teaches patience. A practiced eye can sense where more is needed. But which organs understand the value of restraint. The piece not placed. The imperfection that depicts devotion.

I should like to kneel. To seize and be seized. To witness a summer tanager loosen a prickly fruit. Something shaped like a heart. Not the cartoon kind with even edges. Something three-dimensional. Built like a fist ready to open.

The noise of descent startles. Such fragrant *deshabille*. No one expects intoxication in a stranger's garden. And yet it happens. We rub the white pulp. Exchange tactile certainty. I watch as you touch every piece before you choose where to lay it down.

GUARDIANS TO THE WOUNDED AIR

We sit atop our boards and watch and wait
The faintest roll from a motoring skiff
The only waking sign upon the sea

One gentle swirl of legs or stroke of palm
Will keep us near the sweet spot of the dawning
Swell sensed in skyline ripples stirring

Our bodies know it's time to align
Parallel to the A-frame barn behind
The bending grass upon the shore

Salt-sense moves us to shift onto bellies
Converging cores to coax the pull primeval
So braced we pace the cage of our craving

Peeling peaks push off pumice rock
Jacked up on jagged shelves to greet
The pump and drive of our sidelong slide

Harmonized hunter and hunted
We turn to face the mirroring green canal
Her weather-mother having traveled miles

To meet us here
Where we may walk on waves and so recall
How once we walked on land

BLUFFS OF POINT LOBOS

Stalled in a rock saddle
between leaning massifs
we meet the gale face of ocean
as it seals the narrow col
white frenzy mutes
all but the whinny of water
charging back to sea
reared up on frothy fetlocks
reeling secret lifelines
hidden within the hollow
steed of the bucking brine
still high on hind legs
impatient to heave
its gifts upon the schist and gneiss
of sediment uplifted

we are waiting
waiting for the breakers
the breaking of the riders

beyond their sharp toothed shores
we mark time by the dial of circling wrens
losing track of their wiser than
(what is clock-wise?) airy waltz
confiding to the clouds
to the known path
we cannot return

THE GARDEN OF EDGAR DEGAS
in memory of a black & white tom

at last
April arrives
as advertised
sunbeam songbird
& green careening
on *pointe* in milky slippers
pink jasmine pirouette
the wooden fence
to skirt a rumpled trunk
that irrepressible pepper tree
which weeps its golden pollen
to feed yellow-jacketed wasps
who are not bees
but still seem sweet
going about their business
the work of exuberance is
reason enough for thanks
may I observe to preserve one more?
a *forget me not* for Edgar
the neighborhood cat
who passed in tuxedoed grace
from 18 years among the salvia
to find his tenth life beyond
the riotous flaunt of memory
sure as the bud-heavy wisteria
bouncing now in the brightening light
as if to court the old and tangly rose tree
one more twirl around the garden old girl
how about it — time is fleeting
yet purple is persistent
nearly irresistible
color of courage and yes
I'd love to dance

ENCOUNTERS
for Hieronymus Bosch

To transmute hell and Humpty Dumpty
Stone of folly and the seven deadlies

From thought vessel to wood panel
Working dream-drawn iconography

With brushstrokes more delicate than
Rhetoric risks the poison of verdigris

Bright vermillion's mercury
Lead-tin yellow and masstone white

Also leaden nails sprout beneath
Our feet a golden clearing and a hill

Human industry recedes
To sky the color of your body bent

Scenes of unveiled ornament
A rope that drags, a whip that looms

Whispers of the hustling rabble fallen
Sound that won't survive

The moment is yours
All energy angled towards what is missing

Lost center, broken wing
An image of the other side

When all Fridays were foreign
Our toys were windmill giants

And no one called us strange

MAROON BELLS

for an Aspen Institute forum on "Fearless Leadership"

I was told there would be no math
In this dominion of undressing
Byword and behest *en plein air*
I simply sought a way to see
More by assuming less

Locus stripped down
To natural light and weather of mind
Sensation selecting its own principal
Objects independent of edict or antecedent
Answers tell us so little

When they are ordered
Not felt by the self daring disorder
That is why I come here
To know fear
To fail first

Alone without
Viewfinder to define
Me or the quadrants that divide
Where my trees tower too tall
Their flattened leaves blurred by air

Of mind above these streams so narrow
It is hard to sort sky from shadow and wind shift
Yet no one demands coherence from the painter
Grumbling *what is she trying to say*
This is the question for poets

As if we know much beyond
No one ever is only one
Among meadow and pure possibility
Squeezing tubes in pleasing tones

To accord answers as the absence thereof

We arrange and disarrange
Applications thick or faint to whim
Yet within the sweet solace of freedom
Forgets the bothersome constraint
Of multipoint perspective

The need for paint to acquaint to guide
Another's eye across the geometric plane
Towards some common vanishing point
Such as cliff or horizon
A gestured path

Where we find ourselves
Treading water in the pooled law
Of concurrence
Needing each other
To stay afloat

Past pretending we're immune
We have had this flight before
Now is not the time
For watchwords and euphemism
Sides dividing from each other

Please stop saying you don't understand
Bring your imagination closer
What fools to think we own
Knowing or each other
I drove a train through your mountains

He dug a tunnel in your sea
Sunk the human odds
I am no better than you
Or those we both dismiss

In the gut of the poem

A mousehole
A crawling towards
This – heroes do not exist
Beyond history's peacetime wish

We intersect
Two receding parallel lines
Appearing to converge
We are the tip of the iceberg

AN INVITATION
for Lily Kanter

Arms full we make our way
Through distracted streets
Mindful we must set our feet
Just so as not to risk a tumble

When did the going get hard-bit
On a distant track the hour glass flipped
Days when worry was worlds away
& laughter lay loose as lemons

Free to be squeezed
Honeyed for sharing
Whole neighborhoods
Seeming to sip the same

Song of pure pleasure
Needing no season of greeting
To be together a net
A feeling

Mixed bags in the marketplace
The women begin to work
Their purposeful design
Dropping in each

An everyday golden good
A globe sun sweet
Merchandise of tree and care
With just this

Most simple instruction
Lemonade
Boon friend
I'll meet you there

NOSTALGIA

Hello you say
Today and maybe
I don't know what hollows
The wheels of public discourse
Corrected by a single foot
Pedal press of animals, of traffic, of crowds
Of dark, of strangers, of being left
A lone ear auditing the sea bed's tick
The second hand
Pulls the pot
Higher than outrage
Or patience
A weakening
Walls made thinner
The when of we
Seen-through
Glowing in the jeweled eyes
Of the adolescent cat
Our coiled reflections
At a thirteenth hour
Wax in the melting sand
Crackles a long-gone
Undersong of trees
Words we once knew
How to make

TOTALITY
for Matt Gonzalez

Night fog fuses the dark driftwood
You stacked from dunes and debris
To fashion a raft the sea does not need
But receives it seems to woo
The swift celestial hare
Long frozen at the feet of Orion
Was that you Lepus we'd soon see
Safe from the chase of the Dog Star
Nibbling grass in Charlie's garden
After this night beneath the dome of ancient fates
We bathe our love in the inky bay
Black poem to winter sky

In the morning half-light
A poem nearly white
Feeds the winged horse of summer sky
She eats from your fingers
Squares of raw sugar
Steamy mouth melting an early frost
I leap across the lawn
Arms filled with the pale tines of fallen stars
Careful not to spill
We hold our paper hearts in see-through bags
Geoglyphs of chalk and charcoal
Forever etched in free stone

I bite into almonds
Give their endless moons to you

Tamsin Spencer Smith, 2016.

Tamsin Spencer Smith is a poet, essayist, and painter. Her debut collection *Word Cave* was published by Risk Press in early 2018. Her poems appear in the verse anthologies *Everything Indicates* (Berkeley, CA: Heyday Press, 2012), *Lightning Strikes: 18 Poets, 18 Artists* (San Francisco, CA: Dolby Chadwick Gallery, 2015), *Love in the Face of Everything* (Mill Valley, CA: Tamalpais Press, 2017), and *Reverberations: A Visual Conversation* (Sebastopol, CA: Risk Press, 2018).

Smith was born in Cambridge, England, and grew up in Coconut Grove, Florida. She graduated with highest honours from Kenyon College, for her thesis on Vladimir Nabokov. Smith is a Henry Crown Fellow at the Aspen Institute, where she gives an annual poetry reading. She lives in San Francisco with her son and daughter.

Made in the USA
San Bernardino, CA
14 January 2019